the fire
never goes out

Quill Tree Books is an imprint of HarperCollins Publishers.

The Fire Never Goes Out
195 Broadway, New York, NY 10007.
www.harpercollinschildrens.com

ISBN 978-0-06-227827-2 (trade bdg.) — ISBN 978-0-06-227826-5 (pbk.)

Typography by Catherine San Juan
21 22 23 24 25 EP 10 9 8 7 6 5 4 3 2 1
❖
First Edition

To everyone harboring their own fire
and to everyone lost in the dark.
May you see the sun again.

the fire never goes out

never goes out

a memoir in pictures

noelle
stevenson

Quill Tree Books
An Imprint of HarperCollinsPublishers

It is 2009. You are 17 and you are on fire. You have hair that's cut as short as it will go, and it doesn't bother you when people tease you for looking like a lesbian because you know you're not. You wear bows in your hair and bright colors and dresses over jeans. You know a few things very strongly: that you want a boyfriend, that Jesus loves you, that you can hate the sin and love the sinner.

You want the world to see you and hear you, but you don't know yet what you are trying to say.

It is 2011. You are 19 and you are broken. You don't wear the bows or the colors anymore and you hate everything about the you from 2009. You don't know very many things after all, it turns out. You don't have a boyfriend. You don't have Jesus either, and for the first time in your entire life, you're alone inside your mind. And one cold night, a girl crawled into your bed to stay warm, but you're not ready to think too hard about that yet.

You are trying to tell the world who you are, but they don't seem to understand. So you pick up a pen and you draw.

It is 2012. You are 20 and you are going to live forever. The world is infinite and it is all in your favor. You're sleeping on couches and meeting strangers and drinking beers you're not supposed to have yet and kissing boys, and it all comes so _easy_. You get a tattoo of a star and a boy you like tells you it means you're a lesbian and you laugh about that, but afterward you wear a bracelet over it.

It is 2014 and it is Valentine's Day and you are crying because you know that soon you will no longer have a boyfriend and not only that but you will never have another boyfriend ever again.

It is 2015 and you are 23 and you have been nominated for an award. You are the youngest person to ever be nominated for that award, but you find yourself crying in the bathroom. Everyone has been so kind to you and you don't want to disappoint them. You are tired and you are alone. Now when people call you a lesbian you don't correct them, but the word feels strange in your mouth. It turns out that kissing girls is just as easy as kissing boys, but for some reason you can't kiss _her_ and you don't know why and you can't stop thinking about it.

It is 2016 and you are on fire. You hope you will be the one she kisses at midnight, but when she does, everything changes. You explode like a firework and your heart breaks violently and out of the pieces something beautiful grows. She folds little paper birds for you and you make bread together, and you've never been so happy. The world has never been brighter. The world has never been darker. You wear black to Pride and you cry uncontrollably at the joyful music. You worry that they will end it just as you are beginning.

The next day, you tell the world who you are, and you never look back.

It is 2018 and you are 26 and you are so, so tired. The fire keeps burning, but your insides have turned to ash. There are blisters on your feet and a rattle in your breath, and every night the end of the world plays out in front of your wide-open eyes. You are going to fail. You are going to let everyone down. Your rabbit heart is breaking against your ribs and you are starting to suspect that you will not survive it.

It is 2019 and you are alive.

The cells of your body are dying and growing again every day, and you are always in the process of becoming something new. You're not sure yet who you will be, but you are ready to find out. You know some things a little better now, and your rabbit heart has grown steadier, and you are learning to be gentler to that soft girl with the bow in her hair who is still somewhere inside of you.

This is her story. This is my story.

2011

2

I have no idea what happened to that cake.

holy ghost

you realize suddenly in the middle of it all

you don't know why but you just go and leave your friends

and you cry once you're outside because you know you can never go back

and you drive away until the city lights drop away behind you

you find yourself at the foot of a hill

so you climb because you need this

there are some deer nearby

and yet you are alive

and it seems to you that that's a miracle

(even if there's no such thing as miracles)

so you go back

and when you get back

no one notices that you were gone

and no one notices that you're any different

and no one notices

that you'll never be the same.

sophomore year

 I have a demon inside of me

 Most of the time I'm fine

 until

 i'm not

 ask me what's wrong help me

 what's wrong? LEAVE ME ALONE

 ha ha ha

listen to them
they don't even know
anything's wrong

having fun without me

you could go have
fun with them
just say you're
sorry
let go of your pride

No

I needed to destroy something
but I didn't want to make a mess

they
were just
scratches
welts
I didn't want
to bleed

they faded
by the end of
the day

I just wanted
an outward
sign that
something was
wrong with
me —
so it wouldn't
be my fault.

9

people kept dying

not even people
I knew well - kids from high school
but I spent
hours on their
memorial
Facebook pages

I'm going to miss you.
You were a good friend.
P.S. You made an A on that test
that you were so worried about.

sob

I started walking out
of church.

I couldn't believe
anymore
but the other
option was
unthinkable.

there were good
times too
like the time
we built a fort in the
common area

and we watched
21 Jump Street inside

and once
we made a huge
bowl of vegan
cookie
dough
and we
ate all of it
instead of making
cookies

and the
painting of
Edward Cullen
I found at a
thrift store

decorated with
real glitter

and the perfect
fall day where we
went apple picking

"What happened to her?"

"I thought she dropped the class."

"No. she jumped in front of a train!"

"she's dead."

death.

in the end it was the concept of the afterlife that broke me.

I can't believe in Hell. What kind of Just God would punish people infinitely for a finite Crime?

Heaven doesn't seem too great either.

Animals don't go to heaven when they die. computers and robots don't go to heaven. why would I?

But it wasn't my own death that scared me the most.

there was an infinite amount of time before I was born where I was unable to think or be.

why should it be any different after I die? why SHOULD my consciousness continue?

It all came down to one day in church.

my dad
will die

my parents —
my whole family

they will die
and they won't
go anywhere

they
will just
stop existing

BATHROOMS

≥CLICK≤

≥sob sob sob sob≤

I stayed in
there for the
rest of the
service

I went back one or two
more times but I could
never quite sit through
an entire service again.

13

I lost 20 pounds in a semester.

It felt like slowly disappearing

washing away down the drain

I started to have crippling attacks of shaking & sweating

I tried to wake up my roommate the first time but my teeth were chattering too hard to speak

14

the weight loss was my proof that something was wrong, and I needed something to be wrong.

It's my fault

I confided in an older friend that I might be bipolar.

I've lost 20 pounds without trying

I wish I had what you have then!

I used to cut my hair as short as I could

I wore colorful layers bows in my hair and dresses over baggy jeans

but after sophomore year I let my hair get longer

I wore fewer colors and layers and I threw away the bows.

My meltdowns came once a week.

I pushed my friend

I screamed at her when she was just trying to help

this isn't me it can't be

I'm sick it's bipolar it has to be

sob sob sob

sniff

I'm sorry

because
if it's not

then this is
just me

and I am
awful
and mean
and bad

Mom, I think
I'm bipolar

she didn't agree.

but it
didn't matter
in the end
because school
ended and I
went home,
briefly.

you look
great!

I'm glad
you let
your hair grow
out. It looked
pretty dyke.

you're so
skinny now!

the weird
thing is,
it never
came back.
and I was
okay.
for some
reason.

I moved out of the
dorms. I was going to
share the new apartment
with one of my old
roommates, but she
dropped out instead.
So I lived alone.

on my own,
I could think.
I was empty, but
not in a bad way —
lighter. freer.

I stopped going
to church.
It got easier.

It's sunday and
I'm going to sleep in.

I had lost
things.

but maybe

I wouldn't
miss them

as much
as I thought.

hello
do you
want to date
me check
☐ yes
or
☐ no

(if you check yes
I will look at you
funny and invent
a million reasons
it would never work out)

2011

year in REVIEW

A lot of awesome things happened in my life in 2011! I also drew a _lot_ this year. I was going through my Doodles folder today, and I think it tells the story of my year better than I can. So I decided to compile them into a little backward look at 2011.

In 2011, I took my first Sequential Arts class. It wasn't my first choice, and I almost dropped it. I knew nothing about comics at this point, while my classmates knew all the big names and had been reading comics for years, so I felt kind of behind.

I don't know why I thought this way; I'd actually been drawing comics for years. I was surprised to find that it wasn't actually a super exclusive club, and that there were a lot of different ways to do it.

In 2011, I shaved the side of my head for the first time at a party.

In 2011, I discovered that watching TV while doing homework makes the whole process much more enjoyable. I began watching _Bones_, and started doodling the characters and posting them to Tumblr.

Around this time I started garnering a small following by drawing matadors and lady pirates.

To celebrate, I drew some requests, which opened the gates for fanart. I'd never done much in the way of fanart before, but I was beginning to discover how much fun it was.

In 2011, while watching the Lord of the Rings trilogy for the umpteenth time, I doodled Aragorn, Legolas, and Gimli in modern-day attire, and posted it online.

Within minutes it had over 600 notes, and after drawing the rest of the Fellowship in the same vein I gained nearly a thousand followers in one night. And thus, the Broship of the Ring was born.

I ended up watching the Lord of the Rings trilogy more times this year than any one person should.

In 2011, I got an apartment in Baltimore and lived by myself for a while...
with a ball python as a roommate.

I was working two jobs, one of which was an eight-hour night shift.
Eight hours of wakefulness five times a week gave me plenty of time to
doodle and catch up on TV series.

I drew myself with a hole in the middle a lot. My life was changing, and although I was happy, I couldn't help but feel that I had lost something in a way I couldn't quite verbalize.

yeah, it looks bad, but it doesn't bother me. Not since the edges went hard. It's quite comfortable, actually. And I'm not looking to fill it.

Not yet.

THERE IS A HOLE that I DON'T WANT to FILL, A DEMON I have COME to LOVE

I also didn't wear pants very often. (It was hot.)

25

In 2011, my friend Aimee and I attended the midnight showing of X-Men: First Class. We were drawing fanart almost before we were out of the theater.

I did a couple of quick, loose panel comics about Mystique getting in the way of everything, which set the mold for future Tumblr comics.

It was a good summer for superhero movies. _Thor_ and _Captain America_ got me deeply invested in Marvel characters and excited for _The Avengers_!

In 2011, I had a short sort-of internship in Washington, DC. I wore a blouse and fought my way through DC traffic a couple of times a week. I was also paying my own rent for the first time, and I felt like a proper adult.

hmm yes
stock market

I moved into another apartment before school started. My would-be roommate ended up not coming back, meaning I was living alone again, and I wasn't sure I wanted to. It turned out to be okay, though, as things often do.

In 2011, I survived both an earthquake and a hurricane, both of which proved to be pretty anticlimactic.

what happened

what it felt like

In fall 2011, I was taking 18 credits and classes with Sam Bosma and Kali Ciesemier, meaning that fall 2011 was a semester of very little sleep, not enough of the right kinds of food, and a lot of long Netflix-and-coffee-fueled homework jams.

Weirdly enough, though, I was kind of having a blast. I was the most comfortable with myself that I'd ever been, and without even realizing it, that hole in my middle seemed to be gone.

In short, 2011 was a good year.

2012

oh don't WORRY too much

this is what you wanted

I was talking to my brother about women's attitudes toward their bodies, especially regarding weight/fat, and when he said "most guys don't notice/care about that kind of thing," I tried to explain why it was a lot more complicated than that. I ended up telling this story.

Body image is something that's so hard to talk about, and it's hard to express body positivity without sounding cheesy, false, or overly simplistic. But I'm gonna try. This is only my own experience, and it didn't magically cure me of all my body image issues—but it was a major turning point for me nonetheless.

I thought I knew what a woman's body looked like.

BOMB SHELL ♡

sure, I knew that those women were paid to look like that, and primped & posed & tweaked, but still—

when you only ever see one kind of woman's body portrayed, sometimes you wonder if you might be a different species from them.

Those bodies were my only reference for whether or not my own body was acceptable.

It didn't compare, and so I looked at my body as weird & gross.

ugh I hate my armpit fat

she doesn't look
like the Victoria's
secret models.
She has so
much body hair
she's got flab
and creases and
dimples.

...why didn't
anyone tell me
those things
were beautiful?

But now, no one had to tell me.
I could see.

we drew a
lot of models.
None of them looked anything
like a Victoria's secret model —
they didn't look like me either, or
like each other. why should they try?

I'd always been told we were all beautiful just the way we are. I never believed it.

there are no concave lines on the human body — only overlapping convex lines.

wow

Until now.

all those bodies fit together in infinitely fascinating ways, and the stuff I hated before — thighs and bellies and wrinkles and bulges — now they were the best part.

aw yes! I LOVE drawing armpit fat!

I used to dream
about a little
boy in
striped
pajamas

I had
to save
him
in every
dream

from snakes

tornadoes

floods

until
one night

I couldn't
save
him

I know
who he was
he was my brother
who was never born

I never
saw him in a
dream again

41

sometimes I
think I would
like to have

:ABS:

but I don't
care enough to
actually work out
or
anything

this is how you get abs right

Dishes

year in REVIEW

If you've been following me since the Broship of the Ring in 2011, you know how far I've come in just a little over a year. This blog and the doodles that I post on it end up serving as a scrapbook or diary—so for the second time, I thought I'd compile them into a comprehensive look back at my life in 2012.

Wow, a lot happened in 2012. It was a GOOD YEAR.

In 2012, I signed up for an Advanced Sequential Art class with Joan Hilty. By this point, I was PRETTY sure I dug comics, but this was going to be the final test. I hadn't made a comic longer than four pages, and it had always been an ordeal. I wanted to see if I was really capable of sustaining a longer story in comic form. And I was pretty sure what the project was I wanted to tackle—I wanted to continue Nimona's story.

I'd already done two NIMONA pages in 2011 for another class—over the course of the semester in Advanced Sequential I cranked out sixteen more. Joan was an incredibly supportive teacher with great advice. I streamlined my comic-making process, and realized that yes, I was a comics person forevermore. I could visualize Nimona's story so clearly that I made a resolution: I would make NIMONA a real webcomic and I would finish it.

In 2012, I saw the <u>Hunger Games</u>, made some dumb comics, and got a butt-load of attention for it.

In 2012, I started looking for an internship for the summer. I had no idea where to start, so I took my quest to Tumblr, hoping that I had some followers who could hook me up with a lead. That's how I got in touch with Shannon Watters, editor at BOOM! Studios, who was looking for an intern...and before long I was making plans to fly across the country and spend the summer in LA.

In 2012, I was getting SOOOPER pumped about the Avengers. Due in no small part to the Avengers cartoon _Earth's Mightiest Heroes_, I formed a deep fondness for the Hulk and Hawkeye and drew a lot of fanart of them.

My Avengers fanart attracted the attention of Gallery1988, who invited me to send some art to their Avengers-themed gallery show...a show that was attended by Joss Whedon himself.

I made myself a Hawkeye costume for the midnight showing and I was the only one in the whole theater in costume.

I drew about ten billion Avengers comics and garnered a fair bit of attention for that, too. It ended up bringing Charlie Olsen, a literary agent at Inkwell Management, to my blog—but we'll get to that in a bit.

In 2012, my piece was accepted into the Society of Illustrators student scholarship show!

In 2012, I drew some Pokeymans.

In 2012, I was desperately searching for a place to stay in LA for the summer. It was harder than I had anticipated.

I don't need a house

I am a turtle

I thought I found a place, and then, the day before I was to get on the plane, it fell through. Luckily, my dad had a friend who lived in Santa Monica, and they very graciously let me sleep on their couch in their entertainment room for two weeks until I could find another place. They were very nice to me and I had a great time hanging out with their two young daughters, but frankly Santa Monica TERRIFIED me.

wait no people like this aren't supposed to exist in real life

Fortunately, I found a room to rent in Mid-City, a much less "bougie" part of town, and felt much more at home there. I lived with two USC med students and barely saw them at all.

My internship at BOOM! was going GREAT. They were such a laid-back group of people and I got to look at comics all day, and I loved it.

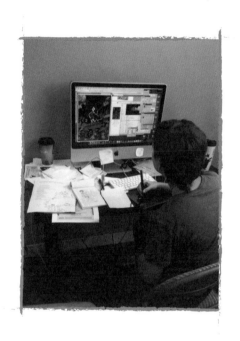

LA was VERY kind to me. I got lots of messages from internet strangers inviting me places, and I'm not sure all of them really expected me to say yes but I was pretty desperate for friends and I ended up meeting loads of new people and EVERY SINGLE ONE OF THEM WAS GREAT. What are the odds of that? From a movie at the ArcLight with Anita Sarkeesian to a Drink-and-Draw at Pen Ward's house, to watching _Jurassic Park_ in a cemetery, to a Bad Robot Fourth of July party, to brunch at the cool hipster joints and comedy shows at Meltdown, I was having a blast and being shown around LA by all the cool Angelenos.

In 2012, I was on my first panel at ALA! We talked about fanart. I attended my VERY FIRST San Diego Comic-Con! It was kind of my first con in general. It was amazing. It blew my mind. I met Michael Emerson.

I was working the BOOM! booth as an intern, but I still had TONS of people come up to say hi, get autographs, and have pictures taken with me. And I got to track down and fangirl over some of my own favorite artists! It was a generally awesome and overwhelming experience.

In 2012, I launched NIMONA as a webcomic, with the help of the great Stephen Warren. It was great. And scary.

As I mentioned before, Charlie Olsen found his way to my blog through my Avengers comics, and found his way to my webcomic through my blog. He contacted me shortly after with the interest of representing me and helping me to get NIMONA in front of some publishers.

In short, summer 2012 was incredible. I'd never lived in such a big city before, with so much happening all the time. Everything that I could have hoped would come out of that summer, did. So it was sad when, at the end of the summer, it was time to go home. The thought of going back to Baltimore and finishing my last year of school was a bit depressing, to be honest. And it really did feel like I was putting down roots in LA. This was everything that art school had prepared me for, after all. But in the end, I did go back.

every day it was sunny and cloudless.

I took my parents up to New York to meet with Charlie and decide whether or not to sign with him. Feeling pretty good about it, I signed with Inkwell Management shortly after that, and moved back to Baltimore for my last year of school.

The rain in Baltimore is cold and bleak.

But at the end of the day, you get to take off the wet clothes

and remember how nice it is to be warm and dry.

Unfortunately, my parents' business was going through some rough times, and their credit suffered. As a result, I was denied my parent plus loan, which was nearly $20,000. I was worried for a while that I wouldn't be going back to school after all—fortunately the school came through for me and scraped up some scholarships, and we made ends meet in the end—with the help of everyone who bought prints from my shop and donated to my comic!!

REASONS TO BUY ART:

packaged for you with artist hands

your walls will look so good

really rad art

help artist's belly eat food

food for artist = more energy to draw art for your amusement!

ARTIST WILL LOVE YOU FOREVER

In 2012, while I was in school, Charlie was shopping me around to publishers in New York—and we ended up striking a deal with HarperCollins. Through a completely unlikely series of circumstances, a chain of events that started in 2011 with a dumb kid and a blog, I had a book deal.

In 2012, I turned 21 at last. In the past few months, I've illustrated the cover to Ryan North's Choose-Your-Own-Adventure Hamlet book, which set the record as Kickstarter's most-funded publishing project, AND Rainbow Rowell's YA novel _Fangirl_ with St. Martin's Press. On January 2nd, you'll be able to buy my very first published short comic, a four-page backup comic in _Fionna and Cake_ #1, from BOOM! Studios! It's almost like I'm a real grown-up person.

It's been an incredible journey, you guys. Thank you so much for supporting me all this way. I couldn't have done it without you <3

2013

First day of weights class

"I can lift these baby weights no problem

woo yeah

the next morning

hop hop

CLUNK

laundry

dump

mmm

#1:

get nakers
or hair will get
in your bra and
that is the
worst

thinning
shears...
good for
hair?
who
knows!

clippers also

#2:

hack away
at bits that
are poofy

#3:

it is your worst
haircut ever.
There's hair
everywhere
and it still
somehow
gets in
your bra.

Holy

Week

you see
yourself
as pretty
harmless,
mostly

but
sometimes
it's like a
door opens
in your
chest

and a thick
black slime
rushes out and
covers your
body and it
transforms
you

you never
knew you
could be
so angry

but then
it flows away
as quick as it
came
    and it's
    just you
    left there

and you see
what you've done

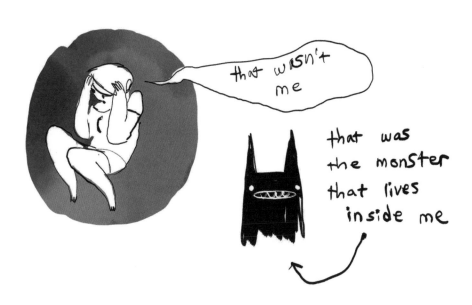

that wasn't me

that was the monster that lives inside me

but the change was so quick and so seamless that you can't help but wonder

if your flesh isn't just the monster's disguise.

I am afraid

of money
of death
of how my hands
   shake all the time

of burning out
   of going up in flames

of there being nothing real inside me
   and that one day everyone will
      be able to see that

year in REVIEW

For the past two years, I've been compiling year-in-review posts on New Year's Eve.

2011 was the year everything started happening.

In 2012, things continued to happen.

So you will be pleased to know that in 2013, _things happened even more._

In 2013, I was working on my last semester of art school. I had become disenchanted with the environment—I was tired of being told what to do and wanted to focus my full attention on my own projects. After the summer I spent in Los Angeles in 2012, I'd felt my life beginning, only to put it on hold for another year to earn what felt like a largely pointless document.

It was always my plan to go back to LA as soon as I finished school, but I knew it was a hard sell. It was on the other side of the country, expensive, and I didn't have a specific reason that I needed to be there, like a job. So when my parents came up to Baltimore for a visit, I ran the idea past them, not expecting an enthusiastic response. To my surprise, my mom calmly and practically told me I needed a plan for how to get there, and helped me figure out some options. Before I knew it, it had become real. I had a plan.

I buckled down for my last semester of senior year, but due to a generous share of senioritis, it wasn't always easy...

I don't want to do this
who wants to go to the bar instead

hooray

I enjoyed the time I spent with my friends senior year, but still, I was ready to go.

All of my mixed feelings toward my school culminated on graduation day, when they called me by the wrong name.

Nicole Stevenson!

It felt like a cruel kick out of the door. I was going to be in debt for what seemed like the rest of my life to pay back nearly 100K in student loan debts in order to have attended school here, and they didn't even know my name.

Student Loans

you better be worth it, little guy

But it didn't matter. I was done, I was gone, I had earned that piece of paper—fortunately with my name spelled right on it. And looking back now that I have some distance, I can see what that school did for me, and how I wouldn't be where I am now without it. My time at art school was filled with extreme highs and lows, but it's where I became an adult.

I had a ticket to fly to LA only a week after graduation. I couldn't bring much with me—only what I could fit in two suitcases. I was starting to get nervous—California was so far away! What if it wasn't like how I remembered it?

But as soon as I stepped out of LAX, I was reassured. It had always felt like a place that I belonged. It was big, exciting, and full of possibilities.

I moved into my new apartment and met my roommate and her two dogs. I bought a car and a bunch of IKEA furniture, and before too long I had begun my new life in LA. I was paying my rent, bills, and car payments by myself. I was making a living off of my art in one of the most exciting cities I'd ever been in—living the dream!

In 2013, I signed with a talent agency in LA, the Agency for the Performing Arts, who specialized in TV and movies. They sent me out for general meetings with all kinds of neat TV and animation studios, which was super exciting!

I went to San Diego Comic-Con with BOOM! Studios for the second time. Despite my body sabotaging me with various illnesses, I had an awesome, if overwhelming, great time.

The summer passed and fall began and for the first time I didn't have to go back to school. It was awesome. I had friends, opportunities, and there was always something cool to do.

Although when it came to dating and relationships, I was in no better shape than ever. It seemed that when it came to romance, my life had been a series of bad timing and being on various sides of unreciprocated interest.

But then, unexpectedly, that changed, and I was amazed to find that maybe sometimes your orbit can line up with another person's just right.

Natasha!
can i help?

oh no! Natasha!

NATASHAAAAAA

In 2013, my art graced the covers of not one but TWO books, as well as an audiobook and a couple of comics.

In 2013, I wrote an episode of _Bravest Warriors_, which will air soon!
   And I worked with What Pumpkin on Namco High.
   And of course, drew some pretty badass moments in my webcomic NIMONA!

...and that's not to mention several secret projects I can't talk about just yet!

In 2013, I won the Slate Cartoonist Studio Prize for Best Webcomic, was nominated for a Harvey Award, and Paste named me one of the top ten comic artists as well as the best webcomic of 2013!

In 2013, I attended comic conventions in New York City, Baltimore, Bethesda, Washington DC, Seattle, San Diego, and Los Angeles, to name just a few!
And finally, in 2013, I turned 22!

2013 was good to me. I'm exactly where I want to be, and I'm so lucky to be supporting myself by telling stories, just like I've always wanted. I'm so excited for 2014—there's still so much to be done!

2014

I am
on fire

literally on fire
all the
time

aaaaahhh

oh my god oh my god oh my god

are you
ready,
baby?

At the airport

year in REVIEW

In 2014, I:
- finished my first webcomic
- got a job writing for cartoons
- had a breakup
- went to a con that turned into a meme
- got a dog!!
- saw some pretty bad movies
- wrote some comics
- worked hard
- grew a lot

2015 is gonna be a big one—in just a few short months my first graphic novel, NIMONA, will hit the shelves! The first _Lumberjanes_ trade will also drop, and you'll get to see my first work for Marvel and DC, along with some other exciting announcements.

I still have so much to learn and so far to grow. Thanks for taking this journey with me, and I hope this new year is a good one for you all <3

2015

is this
what
you
wanted
to be?

clouds

like every kid, I wanted to touch the clouds

to hold them soft as cotton candy lighter than air

to sleep on them

to run across them — to explore their caves and mountains.

but you find
out, soon enough,
that you can't touch
clouds. They're nothing
but condensation, cold
and wet, and not
fluffy at all.

this is what my love for you
is like.

you are nice to see
from my airplane window

but I am safe here.

I can't touch you.
and if I tried, there'd be nothing
there — just coldness, wetness,
a sickening drop.

I know you'll never love me.
That's okay.
That's why I chose you.

I only wanted the desire
and none of the risk.

but there's always a part
of me that doesn't
understand.

doesn't know this
isn't real.

and I dream of flying.

I can touch
the clouds and it's
everything I ever
thought it would be.

you forget it isn't
real.

and
when you
wake up

the ache
you
thought
was gone
is still
there
after
all.

you'll never fly like
that.

and the clouds are only water.

94

year in REVIEW

Is 2015 already over?! How did that happen?

2015 has been the goal year for me for a while. It was the culmination of several years of hard work and rapid climbing, so to see it come to fruition was...well, frankly, terrifying. And amazing, of course. And heartbreaking. And exhilarating.

In 2015, the school project turned webcomic turned graphic novel that I spent more than three years working on was finally published by Harper-Collins. It became a real book you can hold in your hands and buy in a store. It premiered on the New York Times bestseller list.

In 2015, the first trade of Lumberjanes was published as well. It, too, premiered on the New York Times bestseller list.

In 2015, my first published work for both Marvel and DC hit stands: a story in the Thor Annual that I wrote, and a Wonder Woman story that I illustrated. A few months later, my first miniseries for Marvel premiered, a weird little YA high school story set in the middle of the massive summer event Secret Wars, carrying on the title of Runaways.

In 2015, my first TV writer credit hit the air with the premiere of season 2 of Wander Over Yonder.

In 2015, Lumberjanes won two Eisners and a Harvey.

In 2015, NIMONA made the shortlist of five books to be nominated for a National Book Award in children's literature. I was only the 3rd person to be shortlisted for a graphic novel and the youngest ever nominee.

In 2015, both NIMONA and _Lumberjanes_ went on to be optioned as movies.
  2015 was a banner year. And 2015 was one of the hardest, scariest years of my life.

I'd climbed higher and faster than I ever thought was possible, and suddenly I was terrified of falling. I couldn't stop looking down. Ever since art school, I was afraid of burnout. Burnout was final. Burnout was a death sentence. And in 2015, I officially burned out.

But, well, I got better?

ok, so maybe you ARE burning out.

Maybe that's okay.

I'll rise from the ashes like a PHOENIX

and I'll be way hotter

In 2015, I stepped down from a project that was and remains very dear to me...and was one of the most exhausting, emotionally draining projects I've ever worked on. The choice to depart was entirely mine, and it was entirely the right thing to do. I needed to get better, and that meant certain things needed to be left behind.

I think it's time that you Shed your skin and climb out of the hole you have dug yourself in

here's your second chance.

what will you do?

In 2015, I moved out of the apartment where I lived alone and moved into a house in a quiet neighborhood with a roommate. And thus began the era of Galhalla.

Galhalla became a place of healing, of gathering, of commiseration and support, of lights and music and movie nights and way too much take-out Indian food. It became a safe place, a place to take pride in. It represented a fresh start to me.

I thought I'd been strong before, but I'd been isolated and closed off. I thought being strong meant being as hard as diamonds and never letting anyone get close enough to hurt me. And to be sure, my faith in others was shaken a lot in 2015.

do you remember being young

and so on fire with the idea of love that you went dancing and singing through the house

and all the stupid little things mattered so much

you grew
up, but not
really.

you fell in love so fast.

that was the
last of your
childish
loves

before your
soft baby
heart
crystallized

you moved on
and you were fine.

you were
hard as
diamonds.

and before too
long you discovered
what it was
like to be on
the other
side

they liked
your sharp,
hard, shiny
crystals.

so did you.

you thought
maybe if you
acted it
out

you would feel the
fire again

but you never
did

did you actually
want to?

why are you doing
this anyway?

Your heart
doesn't feel
broken. You
just feel
guilty.

the
truth is, you don't
mind being
alone.

you're not a little girl anymore.

you don't want the things you thought you wanted then.

you're fine.

you're hard as diamonds.

But that's not what strength is. The ability to adapt and grow, to let yourself rest, to ask for help when you need it...that's real strength. And I grew so much in 2015. I feel every day that I'm becoming more and more the person I was always meant to be. I've learned to identify the things that are most important to me and focus on those things, and I've learned to let go of the things that just don't make the cut.

There's no way 2016 will be as flashy as 2015 was, but that's fine with me. I'm ready to put my head down and get back to work. There are so many things I still want to do and I'm nowhere near done. I'm stronger, I'm calmer, and I've learned a lot. There are still so many stories to tell.

I'm still afraid, but it doesn't stop my heart anymore. Occasionally, I sleep through the night. And I have a lot of great people by my side to help me. I'm learning to put away the diamond exterior and let people get close again. To be good up close instead of just from a distance. I'm letting myself be happy.

a change is coming,
I can feel it

the air
is heavy
with it

I think i'm
falling

but i don't
care

So here's to you, 2015. Thanks for giving me so many great things and for kicking my ass in the process.

I'm 24 today. So bring on 2016. Let's make some stories!

2016

they say that
red birthmarks show how
you were killed in a
past life

i have a
small one

just over
my heart

i wonder how
it happened

Track 1
Riptide (the Taylor Swift cover)

you were bold, & young, &
drunk on loneliness.

you were pretty good
at kissing girls

and pretty good at waking
up alone.

you didn't mind.

your cruel young heart liked the taste of
blood, & it was better for it to go hungry.

but you never saw her coming.

you crashed
into
each
other

so
slowly

and
so hard.

In the morning, she was still there.

your cold young heart was afraid
and you ran.

Track 2
Do I wanna know? - Arctic Monkeys

there were cracks in your
hard baby heart.

you couldn't stay away.

Oh, you knew it was a bad idea.

but it kept happening.

you never slept at all those nights. You didn't want to miss anything.

and what do you do with a shooting star?

you make a wish.

oh baby, you're in too deep.

Track 3 -
Don't Go - Allison Weiss

 she left
a toothbrush
at your place.

~~it gave you hope.~~

you tried not to hope.

~~you wished she could just stay for coffee.~~

you knew better
than to wish.

~~you wanted her to just be with you.~~

no.

you knew how this worked.

Track 5 -
Friday I'm in Love - The Cure

Track 6 -
Wait For Me — Allison Weiss

you never were good at
staying away from
each other.

I'm excited to
decorate a
place of my own

you helped her
pick things out for her
new apartment

what if —

not yet.

Track 7
wherever is your Heart - Brandi Carlile

you made me feel like
I was always falling

always falling down
without a place to land

somewhere in the distance
heard you calling

oh it hurt so bad
to let go
of your
hand

we doing this?

yeah

wherever is your heart

I call home

year in REVIEW

You know, I almost didn't think I was going to do one of these this year! After a year of quietly working away on various secret projects, it felt like I didn't have a lot to show. And the world after November 8th feels like waking up from a hopeful dream to realize that everything's been fucked for a long, long time, and it's likely to get worse. So how could 2016 have been a good year? But to be honest... 2016, while complicated, was one of the happiest years I've ever had.

Literally the first thing I did in 2016 was fall in love with someone I shouldn't have. Still, as someone historically terrible at being in love, it was easy to push aside any misgivings and self-preservation instincts I might have and just fall, hard.

I'd always had an idea of myself as a very emotionally tough person who was at best incredibly skeptical of romance. I liked being single, and I was good at it.

I was
as hard as diamonds.

bright & beautiful
and untouchable.

I wasn't always like that.

how strange
to have such pride
in the part
of myself that
seemed to be
missing

But something had started to change in me. After throwing myself entirely into my work for several years and seeing it pay off in a big way in 2015, I was tired. And I was scared. And it was hard to see exactly what I was working toward when it seemed like I risked going up in flames when I'd only just begun.

the fire
never
goes out

sometimes it
keeps you
warm

sometimes it
makes your
blood run
cold

It turned out I wanted more. I loved my work, but I wanted something that could love me back.

I started losing a lot of sleep-partially from stress, and partially because what had started as an uncomplicated crush was quickly spiraling out of control.

I have trouble falling asleep sometimes.

The best solution I've found is to listen to November Rain in bed.

It's almost 10 minutes long. Usually I fall asleep before the last big guitar solo. If not, I start it again.

I dunno. It's soothing.

January seemed to last a million years. Nothing that happened next was pretty.

for all
    the walls
    I thought I
        had
not a single one held.

perhaps they'd never
been so strong.

go to sleep

you didn't do anything
wrong.

you didn't.

right?

just

go to sleep.

And then, it was over.

your bed isn't
growing any colder

or any more empty.

your broken heart
still beats.

Except it wasn't. Because we just weren't smart enough to let it be.

but in my softness
I was as strong as I'd
ever been.

and I

reached

again

for your hand.

January was finally over, and suddenly I wasn't alone anymore. And cautiously, we made our way forward.

Simple things

- a root beer float

- a toothbrush

- a tiny dog trying to walk in the tall grass

shhhhh shhhhhh

- the sound of waves

I'd like it
if you stayed

The next few months were some of the happiest that I can remember.

135

Also in that time, I visited Skywalker Ranch, won an Eisner, and got a new job, one with my very own office, working on something that I am SO, SO excited for everyone to see!

But as 2016 has shown me in so many ways, nothing is ever simple.

June 12, 2016

"they say there was a shooting in a gay club. 20 dead at least."

we wore black to Pride

(My First Pride)

Has it always been so
bad?

probably.

I was just too
foolish to see it.

I'm 20
and I'm
going to
live
forever

(July 4, 2012)

Now,
death is everywhere.

It seems
inevitable that we
will tear ourselves
apart but maybe
it has always felt
that way.

drought

fire

death

in schools
in theaters
in churches
in the streets

I think it has probably
always felt like
this.

It had always felt like I'd inherited a good world, a world that had no choice but to keep getting better, and I would surely benefit. As the year wore on, that illusion was shattered again and again.

So here we are. 2016 is over, and no one knows what's going to happen next. It may be that 2016 is the best year I'll see for a while, but I'm not giving up, and I'm not alone.

Thanks, everyone, for coming with me this far. It's time to wake up and it's time to fight. I hope we'll all be okay in the end, but I won't leave it at hope anymore. I'm grateful for the good things I have, and whatever 2017 has in store, I'll try to be ready.

2017

try to be
calm

your fear of doing wrong
is keeping you from
doing good.

this is what
you wanted

ain't
you proud?

you're
not
evil

you are a
mundane, selfish
kind of bad
and that is
what you're always
feared, isn't it?

you do kind things
for praise

or to feel
better

you fear hurting people

but maybe because you
fear being disliked.

you're not strong
or brave
in the way you
want to be

you wanted
to be seen

it only
made you more
lonely.

to be loved

you are
a goat among sheep

weeds among wheat

a vessel destined
for destruction

It's what they
always said you were.

oh child, they'll
never love you.

I have
so many
good things

they are
what I always
wanted

so I
cannot admit
that they are
destroying me

I want to
be stronger
than this

but
I don't think
I have it as bad
as most

I have always
been able to
stand up again

Easter 2017

happy Easter! How are you?

I'm good!

how is Molly?

?!

She's good!

does grandma know Molly is my girlfriend?

. . .

> iMessage

yeah she's not that naive!

I've never been good at having secrets

150

I feel like I'm going
crazy when I have
to keep something inside

but sometimes
it is the unselfish way

oAllowed on Timeline
LA Pride 2016 —
with Noelle Stevenson

Write a comment...

I think she figured it out
after that picture of y'all
at Pride

she took it really well

my little
Noelle

I can't believe he's really gone

before my opa died he asked me

are you happy?
do they accept you?

I didn't know what
he meant.

He didn't even remember
my name at the time.

but I said

yes, opa,
they do.

It's nice to not have a secret anymore

OTTMAR "OTTO" R.
WEMMER
DEC 1 1930
JAN 27 2017

year in REVIEW

I miss being you sometimes.

Me? I'm a mess. I'm hungry and lonely and cold all the time because the radiator doesn't work and I'm scared of the landlord. And I never sleep.

Yeah. I guess you'll miss that one day.

You'll miss when the world could be anything, and anywhere is better than here.

I'm proud of you. I know you've waited so long to hear someone say it. You fought your way out of the dark.

I will too.

2018

Love letter to a D&D character

My first D&D character was a pretty typical first D&D character: a chaotic evil teen tiefling warlock

She gave me the chance the explore melodramatic, messy, angry feelings I'd always felt but had no outlet for

but ultimately, she brought something out in me I didn't like - something full of rage & insecurity

so in our
new campaign, I
chose a new kind
of character:

Quorrin, middle-aged
halfling sorcerer.

she was a washed-up
former child star &
recent divorcee
looking for a
fresh start.

but
no sooner
had she
embarked on
her new career,
than she and her new companions
were cursed by a demon
that would eventually
destroy them

Still, she
didn't let it get her
down. Determined to
"say yes to life,"
Quorrin did
her best to
take care of
the group,
electing herself
"the mom"
despite being
vastly unqualified

163

Quorrin embodied both the traits I envied and the traits I feared. what is it like to rebuild your life after so many disappointments, even when you're afraid?

Knowing it was probably her last journey Quorrin threw herself into adventures like she'd never had before

In the end,
Quorrin was
ready to die

especially
if it
would save
her friends.

as the curse took hold,
knowing that the
world would only ever
remember them as monsters,

the former child
star who had once
dreamed of one day
playing the tragic
female lead

devoted herself to
keeping a careful

record of their stories.

but in the
end, what she had
    to learn to do was
              live...

                    and this
                  time, really

                  say yes
                to life.

Evolution

year in REVIEW

It's been a big year with several big triumphs. The show I've been working on for three years finally premiered, and I got engaged to the best girl in the world. I've never felt more lucky, proud, and loved...but I had another, more personal and harder won victory this year, and I'd like to talk about that first.

This is about mental health, and it's long. Minor trigger warning for things related to that.

I do these posts every year, and have since 2011. Some years, including last year, I wasn't sure if I should continue doing them. The posts encouraged a narrative that I disagreed with as much as I desperately sought to live up to it: that my accomplishments and my youth gave me value, that I was always on the upward climb, that burnout was an easily resolved footnote, that I was young and sharp and <u>fine, I was fine</u> and I would always be fine.

19-24
amazing baby
does a good
job! wow!

25-29
enterprising young
professional, we are
so impressed &
proud

30+
dead I
guess

Noelle
died from
cartoons
oops

It was as shortsighted as it was unsustainable. The truth was, something was wrong and had been wrong for a long time.

At the start of the year, and when I made last year's comic, I was already close to hitting the wall. I had thrown myself into work, and the show, and I was losing myself in it. I wasn't sleeping. I no longer felt any connection to my own body.

you don't know what
your hair is doing now

none of it feels like
you. But it
is growing.

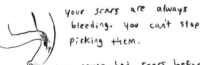

your scars are always
bleeding. you can't stop
picking them.

you never had scars before
but they feel right now.

your face no
longer looks
familiar

your words no
longer feel like
your own.

I was doing everything right, I thought: I was working out, going to ther-
apy, taking breaks, I had an incredibly kind and patient partner who was
always there for me. I didn't understand why I couldn't just, through force
of will, make myself okay.

I was burning through energy stores that I didn't have, and I knew it
but I couldn't stop. There was something in me that wouldn't let me.
I identified it commonly in my drawings as a fire. I'd felt it for years, at
varying levels of intensity, but now it seemed that it was burning out of
control and it was going to take me with it.

do you even remember a time when you didn't feel like you were on fire

whether it lit you up

or burned you apart

It keeps you warm.

It eats you alive.

It made me feel like I was living my life in a perpetual state of fight-or-flight—usually fight. At first, my fierce and stubborn temperament was a benefit in the environment I was in. It was clear to me that showing weakness, even for a moment, would be the end. But it was hard to know when to stop fighting, and fighting takes its toll.

you are not
strong

just stubborn.

your
scales are
sharp.

your fire
burns hot.

you can inflict
hurt without
even trying.

but
you are fragile.
your bones break
so easily and
they never
quite heal.

who will care
for you when
your fire turns
to ash?

What do you want, sympathy?

are you going to pretend you haven't tasted blood and liked it?

Could you use your scales to protect instead of hurt?

Could you control your fire so it warms instead of destroys?

The show was everything to me, and it was hard to see beyond it. I was keenly aware of how lucky I was to be a showrunner, but I also took the success of the show and the well-being of the crew incredibly personally, and so the guilt of _letting everyone down_ convinced me that I was not allowed to be happy in the role—that it would be irresponsible.

your soul's not gone

it's just not in your body anymore.

you let the wolves have it, but it's okay.

Each bite you feel a little less.

It will leave a scar. You don't know how bad yet.

Don't look down.

this is not your hair

or your chest

or your arms

or your voice

your eyes go flat so often.

I'm sorry.

You can do it.
You are sturdy.

You will be everything to everyone.
You will make it to the end.

Then maybe you will get your body back.

and maybe, when it heals, it will be beautiful.

I was so tired, but the fire was still there, and it propelled me stubbornly forward even as it consumed everything inside of me. I thought I could fix everything if I just _tried harder_...and if I didn't fix things, no one would. I lived in constant dread of the one small slip or mistake that would ruin everything forever. I carried it all, in obsessive detail, in my head, and eventually I stopped being able to turn it off.

Admitting that something was wrong would mean that there was something wrong with _me_—that I hadn't done a good job, that I wasn't cut out for this, that I had failed. So despite all the red flags, I just kept pushing through.

And my body started to fail.

I think I am destroying myself

my hands shake

sometimes I cannot feel them at all

hhh

I forget to breathe or I cannot breathe at all

I can't stay awake

I can't stay asleep

sometimes I can only see the

edges of my eyes

and I cannot understand your words

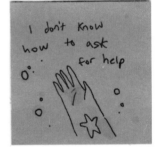

I don't know how to fix it

I don't know how to ask for help

I'm sorry I am trying

this is not how I wanted to be

For so long I'd put all my personal value in my success, as much as I knew that I shouldn't. I had climbed so high, never really stopping to rest, and I was _so scared_ of falling—I didn't think I'd survive it.

I didn't know that falling was exactly what I needed.

almost
everyone who dies

dies on the
way down.

here's
what they
don't tell you about
climbing
mountains

the summit,
as much as
you want
it,

is only the
halfway
point.

and night
     will be here soon,

          and there will be no way
          to go but down,

                    and you will
                       be so tired.

will you
fall in
plain sight,

a monument

to those

who come

after

you?

will you
vanish into
the darkest depths,
never to
be seen
again?

I won't get into exactly what happened—maybe another time. But it was brutal, and swift, and merciless. This was it, the thing I'd been most afraid of. I was going to be assigned the label of "difficult woman," another one who just couldn't take the pressure.

My self-image shattered. But the truth was, there hadn't been much left of it to begin with.

And finally I knew what I had to do.

you
have
broken

but you
will not

stay
broken.

There's something strangely calming about the fire outside becoming hotter than the one inside. I got back up, put on nice clothes, and stood my ground.

It turns out there can be freedom in the falling, and strength in the breaking.

And finally...I sought out help.

you're not okay,
   but you will be.

you are not
done fighting
       yet

+ you will see
   the sun
        again.

I saw a psychiatrist and finally got a diagnosis I'd needed for a long time.

Everything fell into place.
   The diagnosis alone was a huge relief. It offered <u>context</u> for my rac-
ing mind, twitching fingers, the long sleepless nights, the pervasive dread
and surging panic, the darkest hopeless lows and vibrating burning highs.
I wasn't just falling apart. This was something I could <u>face</u>, and manage.

I went on medication.

I had always been afraid of medication. It was easy to romanticize the fire in my brain, and internalize the pervasive notion that it was what made me strong, interesting, creative, and that medication would take that away. It took being pushed to my breaking point to realize that it wasn't worth it.

spite is a powerful motivator

anger is a poison

It would have been worth it anyway, but being on medication has in no way lessened my capacity for feeling or creating. It's made creating _easier_—it's made my feelings stronger and more sure because I know that they're real. I can see myself again. The face in the mirror is mine. I know what I want, and what I need, and I trust myself for the first time in a long time. The joy of creating has come back.

It was not the diagnosis or the medication alone that helped me get better. I was carried through the darkest parts by the strength of those around me—my awesome and powerful coworkers, the women who kindly mentored me when I sought them out for advice, and the care and love of the most wonderful girl in the world.

when I am feeling very bad, usually I'll latch onto some song extra hard.

♪ I can see clearly now the rain is gone ♪

I like this song because it doesn't pretend things are going to be easy.

♪ I can see all obstacles in my way ♪

at some point, it started to feel true.

♪ gone are the dark clouds that had me blind ♪

it's gonna be a bright bright sunshiney day.

I'd seen the sun before, but it was different this time. I'd made it through my worst fears, and it hadn't killed me. I could do it again if need be. A bad situation had worked out all right in the end, but even if it hadn't, I would have been okay. I wasn't reaching my expiration date as a young creator—I was maturing, building the strength, real strength, to live the rest of my life.

take a breath,
as well as you
can

and prepare for
the careful climb
down.

you have a long life
still to live

and many more
mountains to climb.

love your younger self

and let them die.

This isn't a resolution, a happy ending—it's the beginning. I will still struggle, and fall, and break, again in the future. There will be highs and lows, and the fire is something I'll have to carefully manage for the rest of my life. But the places I've been broken will not break so easily in the same way again.

It's been a hard year, an ugly year, a long year.
It's been a good year.
On to the next.

2019

it has been
a year
since
it all came
crashing
down.

my hair is getting
pretty long.

each inch

is a
reminder

that I
made it

this far.

I try not
to pull out
the strands.

my arms
are getting
stronger.

I try not to
pick the
skin.

I use my lungs
to breathe.

at night
I close
my eyes,

and in the morning I will
open them again.

my flame
burns
soft
& warm.

take a breath,
as well as you can.

turn your face toward
the light.

it is time for the
next step of your journey.

My dad always said we would all get married in the old family church

I never had any feelings about that until I realized I was no longer welcome there.

at first, it was a relief.

Noelle + ??? we are all so proud

like a knot of dread that I had been born with had suddenly unraveled.

So, when is it your turn?

maybe never!

but
then

don't laugh, okay?

I haven't worn a dress in years

I know it looks dumb

I thought I'd left all this behind.

I thought I'd been okay with that.

maybe it's okay to
want this, after all.

Every cell in my body has died and grown again

acknowledgments

To my wife (wife!!) Molly—you are my light in the darkness and an inspiration to me, always. I can't wait for the rest of our lives together.

To Mom and Dad, Grandma and Opa, Alex, Hannah, Gracie, and Jacob—I love you and you'll always be a part of me. Don't let this book make you worry too much!

To Andrew and Charlie—you believed in me before anyone else did. Thank you for giving me this chance to tell my story.

Thank you to Cat San Juan and Erin Fitzsimmons for designing such a beautiful book!

To Aimee, my rock when I was adrift at sea—that salad saved me in more ways than you know.

To the Taylors—you're always in my heart no matter how far apart we are!

To Grace and Nicole—thank you, and I'm sorry.

To Ms. Hendrix, who fought for me to get an arts education even if it meant teaching two classes at the same time—I wouldn't be here without you!

To Team She-Ra—working with you has been the honor of a lifetime. Thank you for defending and believing in me.

To Lacey—thank you for your mentorship that helped me pull through an impossible situation. I couldn't have done it without you.

To all my friends who have given me a listening ear, a shoulder to cry on, or just quiet solidarity—I am so fortunate and grateful to have you in my life and I hope to always be the friend you deserve.

To Winston, Toast, and Fig—you're pets and you can't read, but thank you for your companionship that has comforted me through so many gray skies and cold nights.

To all the fans and readers who have supported me and encouraged me over the past eight years—you can never know how deeply grateful I am to you. You changed my life—thank you so much.

credits

Photos on pages 1, 26, 33, 53, 54, 59, 81, 89, 96, 107, 123, 135, 143, 161, 185, 187 courtesy of the author.

Photo on page 193 courtesy of Jamie Thrower / Studio XIII Photography.

Images on pages 48 and 54 previously appeared in Noelle Stevenson's NIMONA, 2015.

Page 98:
"Second Chance"
By Dame, from the self-titled album "Dame" (c) and (p) Dame 2004 released by Lujo Records
Lyrics reprinted courtesy of Lujo Records

Pages 118-119:
"Friday I'm In Love"
Words and Music by Robert Smith, Simon Gallup, Paul S. Thompson, Boris Williams and Perry Bamonte
Copyright (c) 1992 by Fiction Songs Ltd.
All Rights in the United States and Canada Administered by Universal Music - MGB Songs
International Copyright Secured All Rights Reserved
Reprinted by Permission of Hal Leonard LLC

Pages 121-122:
"Wherever Is Your Heart"
Written by Brandi Carlile, Tim Hanseroth & Phil Hanseroth
Published by Atlas Music Publishing on behalf of Southern Oracle Music LLC (ASCAP)

W9-CML-185

Contents

Welcome to This Book

National Archives (NARA)

Does watching baseball sound like science to you? What about singing with birds? Or how about eating bugs? It does to the scientists in this book.

One goes digging up bodies in graveyards. Another doesn't just study grasshoppers, she has them for lunch! Call them weird, but these scientists found out some pretty interesting stuff.

Want to know what happens when you mix weirdness with science? Read on.

Target Words
These words help describe how scientists work.

- **discovery:** the act of learning new facts and information

  Jack Farmer hopes that a new discovery will prove that there is life on Mars.

- **investigate:** to search for answers to a mystery

  James Starrs investigates crimes from the past.

- **theory:** an idea or a statement that explains how or why something happens

  Adriana Ocampo has a theory about why dinosaurs died off.

Reader Tips
Here's how to get the most out of this book.

- **Subheads** A subhead is like a title for a section of a book. It tells the main idea. Look at the subhead, "Food of the Future," on page 7. What will this section be about?

- **Fact/Opinion** As you read, try to separate the fact from the opinion. A fact can be proven. An opinion is a feeling or belief.

1

The Insect Eater

Forget beef or chicken, Florence Dunkel says insects are the food of the future.

Welcome to one weird dinner party. Have a seat. Your host for the evening is Florence Dunkel. She's an entomologist. That's a scientist who studies insects.

Hope you're hungry. Dunkel has fixed a special meal just for you. Let's start with some salad. What's wrong? Oh, those crunchy bits? They're just fresh termites.

The main course? A grasshopper stir-fry. Mmm, the meat is so tender. Could you pass the bread and ant jelly, please?

For dessert, we have a special treat, chocolate chirpy–chip cookies. Those roasted crickets taste just like nuts! Please, help yourself to another one.

Okay, Dunkel knows what you're thinking. Termites! Grasshoppers! Crickets! Gross! Who would eat insects?

Well, Dunkel, for one. She has cooked or tasted each of these dishes. She's dined in the world's best insect restaurants. And she's shared bowls of bugs from Mexico to Mali.

Sure, Dunkel likes the taste of grasshopper. That is, after she pulls off the chewy head and legs. But she's also eating for science. Dunkel **investigates** how people use insects as food. She watches how they raise, cook, and eat bugs. And she studies how **nutritious** bugs are to eat.

Food of the Future

Dunkel started this creepy-crawly diet for a reason. Animals such as cows eat a lot of grass. That means they need lots of grazing land. Many countries don't have enough good land. They can't produce enough food. So the people go hungry.

Dunkel thinks insects are the answer. If people ate bugs there would be plenty of food. After all, insects are everywhere. Just look around your basement or backyard.

Eating insects may seem strange to you, but in many countries it isn't weird at all. In Mexico, markets sell grasshoppers by the pound. Colombians grind up ants. Then they spread them on bread like jelly. And in some places in Asia, people eat roasted waterbugs.

"Insects are the food of the future," Dunkel says. "They are healthy. They are **plentiful.** And they are delicious."

But some insects can give you a stomachache. The monarch butterfly, for example, is filled with toxins. Those are poisons that can make you sick. But there are 1,500 kinds of **edible** insects. Most are full of vitamins and minerals. A one-ounce serving of grasshopper has the same protein as a three-ounce piece of steak.

Bug Lover

Dunkel has always liked insects. And not just as snacks. Growing up, Dunkel would take a book down to the nearby lake. She'd come home with a bunch of worms to show her parents. "They never said 'Eeek,'" she remembers. "They always said, 'Isn't that cool?'"

© Peter Menzel

Florence Dunkel says, "Insects are the food of the future."

So bugs have never grossed out Dunkel—even when she ate her first bagful. While studying in Africa, she bought a bag of brown locusts. A cook fried them in butter. She's been hooked ever since. "If people could get over the yuck factor, they'd learn to love insects," she says.

In fact, you've probably eaten bugs yourself. You just didn't know it. Tiny weevils sneak into flour bags. And slimy maggots hide out in cans of tomato paste. In other words, if you have eaten **processed** food, you've eaten bugs.

"Most kids in the world grow up with insects in their diet," Dunkel says. "They laugh when they hear we don't eat them. They say we don't know what we're missing."

Heads Up!

Dunkel says most insects taste good. She also says they are good for you. Which of these statements is a fact and which is an opinion?

2

Detective for the Dead

The murder trail never grows cold for James E. Starrs.

Kearney, Missouri is a dusty farm town. In it sits a lonely gravestone. Beneath the gravestone lies Jesse James. For twenty years, this outlaw robbed trains and banks. But he was shot and killed in 1882. The killer got a $10,000 reward. Jesse James got a lonely grave in Kearney.

Or did he? Some people wonder if James faked his death. That way the law would stop chasing him. Everyone agrees that there's a body buried in that grave in Kearney. But is it Jesse?

The family of Jesse James wanted a final answer. So they called James E. Starrs. Starrs is a world-famous **forensic** scientist. He investigates crimes. If you've got a mystery that's old and a body that's cold, Starrs is your man.

Starrs is known for his work on old cases. He looks into murder mysteries after others have given up. We're talking long after. Most of his cases are older than one hundred years.

You know the first U.S. president, George Washington? Some people said that his brother had been poisoned. Starrs dug up the body. He looked for poisons in the brother's fingernail. Turns out George's brother died of natural causes.

"I'm a voice for the dead," Starrs says. "People say to me, 'They've been gone for so long, why don't you let them rest in peace?' But if it's an unsolved mystery, then they aren't resting peacefully at all."

Digging Up the Past

Starrs got hooked on mysteries when he was a boy. He was sick a lot. He had to stay in bed. Books kept him company. He loved detective stories. He read every Sherlock Holmes mystery.

---**Heads Up!**---

Starrs says he is a voice for the dead. What does he mean by that?

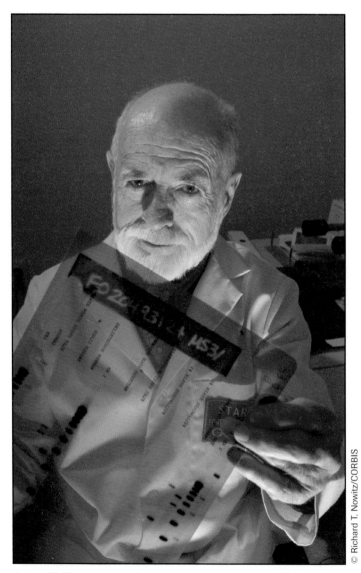

James E. Starrs uses science to solve murder mysteries.

When Starrs got older, he studied criminal law at college. Today he's a professor of law and forensic science. But he's best known for solving age-old mysteries.

Starrs doesn't investigate just any crime. He waits for the family to ask him for help. Then he has to examine the body. Often, that body is six feet underground.

"There's nothing fun about digging up bodies," Starrs says. "It's hard work. It's hot. And, boy, does it smell bad."

In 1995, Starrs went digging for Jesse James. But he soon saw he had a problem. The coffin had broken apart. Bones were scattered in the dirt. "My grandfather was a funeral director, so I got used to being around bodies," he says. "But they were usually in one piece."

In the end, a single tooth from the coffin solved the mystery. Starrs took some **DNA** from the tooth. DNA is found in each cell of your body. Every person's DNA is different, like fingerprints.

Starrs knew that a museum had some of James's hair. He compared the DNA in the tooth to the DNA in the hair. It matched. This proved that Jesse James was buried in Kearney.

"Those are the moments that make it worthwhile," Starrs says. "You are able to give a family an answer about a long-dead loved one. And you are able to finally put a mystery to rest."

Heads Up!

Starrs is a kind of detective. How is his work different from the work of a typical police detective?

3

Take Me Out to the Lab Game

Science is a home run for physicist Paul Doherty.

Here's what most people see at a baseball game. The pitcher goes into his windup. He throws a fastball toward home plate. The batter swings. The ball is hit hard. It sails toward the outfield. Will it be caught? Or will it be a home run?

Here's what Paul Doherty sees. The pitcher twists and turns. He spins the ball as he throws it. This causes it to curve and dive. The batter swings. Energy shifts from the bat to the ball. The white ball soars toward center field. Does it have enough speed to reach the stands? Or will **gravity** cause it to drop into the outfielder's glove?

Huh?

Doherty is not just a baseball fan. He's a scientist, too. He studies physics in San Francisco.

Physics is the science of matter and energy. Doherty says that's what baseball is all about.

Matter is anything that takes up space. That includes the bat and ball. Energy is the power to make things move. That includes swinging a bat.

"Baseball is full of physics," Doherty says. "Think about it. The pitcher uses energy to throw the ball. That batter uses energy to swing the bat. And then there's a **collision,** the whack of the bat against the ball. There's so much energy in that moment. It's like an explosion."

Little League Scientist

For Doherty, it all started in Little League. He played right field. Chasing down high flies wasn't that interesting to him. He mostly wondered why they flew so far over his head. Since then, he's used science to answer weird sports questions.

Heads Up!

Look up collision *in the glossary. Name three sports where two types of matter, like a bat and a ball, collide to release energy.*

Questions like, How fast does a batter have to swing to hit a home run?

According to Doherty, the batter has to think fast. He has about one-sixth of a second to decide if he'll swing at a pitch. "If he has really quick **reflexes,** he can swing in just one-tenth of a second," Doherty says. "That's the difference between a pop fly and a home run."

And why doesn't the ball just keep going up after the batter hits it? The answer is gravity. That's the force that pulls things back to the ground.

But in some places gravity isn't such a big deal. There isn't much gravity on the moons of Mars, for example. There, you could hit a home run every time. "The ball would fly all the way around the moon," Doherty explains. "Then it would hit you in the back of the head."

Training Tips

Doherty thinks science can help people enjoy the game more. It can help them play it better, too. Some pro teams have hired physicists to give them tips.

Paul Doherty sees physics at work when he watches a batter, like Benito Santiago, swing at a pitch.

"No scientist ever invented a pitch," Doherty says. "But they can tell you how one works."

Do curveballs really curve? Yes, says Doherty. The seams on the ball push the air around the ball upward. That makes the ball dive downward.

For Doherty, science is about **discovery** and fun. "Some scientists like to sit in the lab and work on their computer all day," he says. "Me? You can take me out to the ball game anytime."

Heads Up!

Did you know there was so much science in sports? Now that you do, will you think about sports differently?

4

Dinosaur Disaster

Where did the dinosaurs go? Adriana Ocampo looks for answers in the world's biggest hole.

It was a bad day for Earth. In fact, it was probably the worst day ever for our planet. That's what Adriana Ocampo says. She has spent years studying what happened that day. Luckily, it happened 65 million years ago.

"Thank goodness none of us were around back then," she says.

Unfortunately for the dinosaurs, they were.

The worst place to be on that bad day was in Mexico. Well, it's Mexico now. It had no name back then. The morning probably started like any other. The waters were calm. Plant-eating **triceratops** nibbled on tree leaves. **T. rexes** were out hunting.

Suddenly, a rock fell to Earth from space. It was huge. It was a giant **asteroid.**

Small pieces of asteroids hit Earth all the time. They're called meteorites. Most are so tiny we never notice them. But this killer asteroid was six miles wide. And it was moving fast. It flew at the earth at 12 miles per second.

The poor dinosaurs never knew what hit them. The asteroid slammed into the ground. Most of it exploded into small pieces. Dust and rocks flew for hundreds of miles. And that was just the beginning.

The asteroid left a huge crater, or hole. It was 120 miles wide. Today, most of the crater has been covered over by earth and ocean. But that doesn't stop Ocampo.

Dying Days of the Dinosaurs

After years of study, Ocampo has an idea about what the asteroid did to the dinosaurs. And she has put together a **theory** about why they died.

She thinks the asteroid's blast caused earthquakes and huge fires. The impact also kicked up tons of dirt. The dirt hung in the air

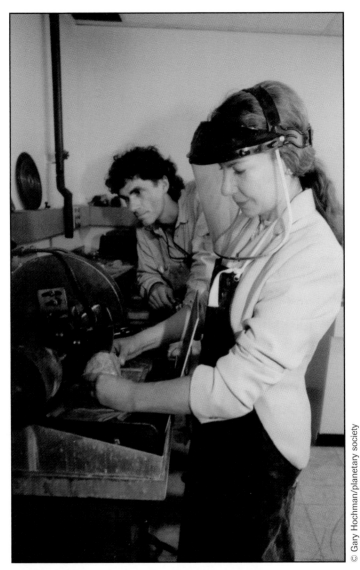

**Adriana Ocampo is a planetary geologist. Her work may have
helped solve the mystery of the dinosaurs' doom.**

and blocked out the sun for months. With no sunlight, the earth became freezing cold. That meant death for both plants and dinosaurs. Most of the animals that **survived** swam deep in the ocean. Or like mice, they lived underground.

Teenage Scientist

Ocampo grew up in Argentina. As a girl, she liked digging in the dirt. She put insects into her pockets. She hid spiders in her sister's dresser drawers. And she dreamed of traveling to outer space. In other words, she loved science.

But in her country, girls didn't have much hope of becoming scientists. So Ocampo's parents sent her to the United States.

When she was just a teenager, she studied with **NASA.** That's the U.S. space program. Now Ocampo is one of the world's top planetary geologists. She studies huge space objects like stars and asteroids.

Ocampo has spent a lot of time around that giant crater. She searches for dirt and rocks from the asteroid's **impact.** One time she was hiking in the jungle. She found a rock the size of a car. It had been thrown in the air by the asteroid crash. And it landed 140 miles away!

Another Asteroid?

Ocampo has figured out where the center of the crater is. It sits under a small Mexican fishing village. Ocampo visited there. She told the villagers about the asteroid.

Many asked the same question. Could it happen again? "It might, in about 40 million years," Ocampo says. "Don't worry. That gives us plenty of time to duck."

Heads Up!

Ocampo's theory is that the asteroid's blast helped kill the dinosaurs. Is a theory the same as fact? What words in the text let you know?

5

Bird Man

This bird-brained scientist sings with his feathered friends.

It's called the dawn chorus. Erich Jarvis loves listening to it. The first time he heard it, he was in the **rain forest** in Brazil.

The sun was coming up. The singing started slowly. A single hummingbird twittered on a tree branch. Then another bird joined in. Then another. Then a hundred more. Soon, the forest was filled with bird songs.

This chorus happens every morning. Some people think it's just pretty music. But Jarvis knows better. The birds are talking in their own language. And Jarvis believes they have something important to say. He thinks they can help us understand the human brain.

Jarvis is a biologist at Duke University. He studies the way living things work. Jarvis' specialty is birds. He likes their beautiful feathers. And he loves watching them fly. But he's really interested in their brains.

"I know it sounds crazy. But these birds have brains that are, in some ways, just like human brains," Jarvis says. "Only a whole lot smaller."

Copy Cats

Humans speak. Birds sing. So what's the connection? Well, some birds use the same parts of their brains to sing as people do to speak, Jarvis says. These birds include parrots, songbirds, and tiny hummingbirds.

He calls them "vocal learners." That means they can learn to copy sounds they hear. That sounds easy, right? It's not. Very few animals can learn to repeat sounds. But others that can are bats, whales, dolphins, and of course, people.

Heads Up!

Jarvis studies living creatures. What kind of scientist does that make him?

Other creatures can learn how to follow commands. "You can train your dog to sit when you say 'sit,'" Jarvis explains. "But you can't teach him to say 'sit.'"

So what makes birds' brains so special? That's what Jarvis wants to understand. That might give him clues about the human brain. "Right now we know a lot more about how a bird's brain works than a human's," he says.

Jarvis hopes his research will help people with language problems. These people might have **learning disabilities.** Or they might have brain damage from an accident.

Bird Music

Jarvis grew up in New York City. The only birds he saw there were pigeons. Now Jarvis spends a lot of time with all kinds of feathered friends. Maybe too much time. Sometimes he sings with them as they fly around his lab.

---**Heads Up!**---

What does Jarvis hope his research will do for people?

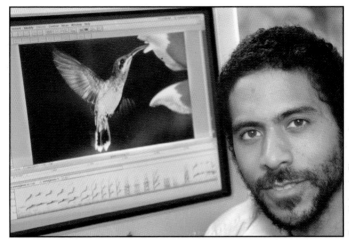

Erich Jarvis thinks this hummingbird sounds a little like Mariah Carey.

Jarvis is mostly a jazz fan. But sometimes he puts on a hummingbird CD. "Everybody has their own music," he laughs. "My daughter listens to J. Lo. I listen to birds."

So which singer sounds like a hummingbird? "Mariah Carey is pretty close," he says. "If she sings any higher, she'll have to get some wings."

6

Is Anybody Out There?

Jack Farmer is looking for life in the universe. First Stop: Mars.

Jack Farmer likes to look up into the clear Arizona night. His eyes find a small bright dot to the south. It seems so close. But really, it's 162 million miles away. He's looking at Mars.

And Farmer wonders, *Is there life out there?*

Farmer is an astrobiologist. That's a scientist who studies life in the universe. He wonders, "Are humans alone in the universe? Is anything living on that dot up there?"

Farmer thinks humans have company in the solar system. And he believes Mars is the best place to start looking. But whatever you do, don't ask Farmer about **UFOs.** He's heard all the jokes. That's natural when you look for life on Mars.

If there is life on Mars, Farmer is sure it won't be little green men. Life on Mars would probably be like germs. They would be too small for the human eye to see.

"We're not looking for dinosaur bones up there," Farmer says. "We're looking for the tiniest building blocks of life."

Looking for Life

Farmer searches Earth for clues about life in space. He collects microbes. Those are things that can only be seen with a microscope. The microbes he's looking for live in rough places. These are spots where most plants and animals can't survive.

If life can make it in these nasty places, why not on Mars? That's Farmer's great hope.

So he looks for tiny creatures in the hot springs of Yellowstone National Park. There they float in boiling water. Or he searches in California's

---

Heads Up!

Farmer thinks there's life in other places in the universe. What do you think?

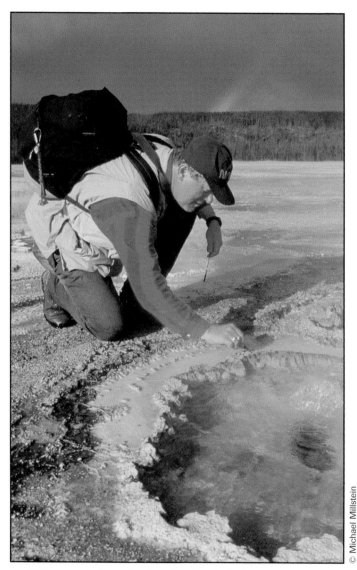

Jack Farmer studies microbes that live in boiling hot places. He wonders if tiny creatures like these can be found on Mars.

Mono Lake. The lake is filled with strong natural chemicals. One drop burns the skin.

Some scientists think Mars is a lifeless rock and Farmer is wasting his time. But that doesn't bother Farmer. He has never followed the crowd. As a kid, his friends traded baseball cards. But Farmer had the biggest rock collection in town. (Okay, it was probably the only one in town.) Farmer also pasted bird feathers into a notebook. He even built a cow skeleton in his garage.

Today, Farmer is a Mars expert. He's also the Vice Chairman of the Native American Advisory Committee at NASA.

Sister Planet?

Mars and Earth aren't so very different according to Farmer. Show him a close-up picture of Mars. He can pick out tall mountains. He can point to places where rivers might have flowed. Life **developed** on Earth, Farmer says. So why not on Mars?

Farmer thinks astronauts will walk on Mars within twenty years. And he thinks Earthlings will live there someday.

But don't load the moving van just yet. We're about 300 years away. That's what Farmer thinks, at least.

Still, Farmer daydreams about a vacation on Mars. He's even picked the spot. It's a chain of canyons called Valles Marineris. It's about 2,500 miles long. And it's more than five miles deep. That's three times deeper than the Grand Canyon.

Farmer imagines standing on the edge of this huge crack. He'd look up into the sky. But this time he'd see a blue dot called Earth. "Man," he'd say, "you can't beat this view."

Heads Up!

How are Mars and Earth alike? How are they different?

They All Laughed ...

... *At Some of the World's Greatest Scientists*

Some were called weird. Some were feared. And some were just ignored.

That's the risk some scientists take when they search for new ideas. But lucky for us, these scientists never gave up, even when the whole world laughed.

Year after year, Wilbur and Orville Wright launched their flying machines. The machines would crash. Everyone laughed. But the Wright Brothers didn't quit. In 1903, they took off again. And this time, they flew. It was a short flight and there was no movie. But it was the first time humans had flown.

Some scientists were even jailed for what they discovered. In the 1600s, Galileo used a telescope to study space. He saw moons circling Jupiter. Impossible, said religious leaders. They believed everything in the sky circled Earth. Galileo said no. Earth was not the center of the universe. Galileo's ideas scared them. So they locked him in his house for nine years. They said they would punish him if he didn't take it back. So he took it back—sort of. But today we all know that he was right.

Glossary

asteroid *(noun)* a rocky space object which travels around the sun (p. 22)

collision *(noun)* when two things crash into each other, often at high speeds (p. 17)

develop *(verb)* to grow (p. 33)

discovery *(noun)* the act of learning new facts and information (p. 20)

DNA *(noun)* the part of a cell that carries one-of-a-kind information about each living thing's body; stands for deoxyribonucleic acid (p. 14)

edible *(adjective)* safe to eat (p. 8)

forensic *(adjective)* relating to law or crime (p. 11)

gravity *(noun)* the force that pulls things down to the surface of the earth (p. 16)

impact *(noun)* the striking of one thing against another thing (p. 24)

investigate *(verb)* to search for answers to a mystery (p. 7)

learning disability *(noun)* a problem that makes it hard for someone to learn (p. 28)

NASA *(noun)* stands for National Aeronautics and Space Administration (p. 24)

nutritious *(adjective)* being full of nutrients or substances the body needs to stay healthy (p. 7)

plentiful *(adjective)* existing in large amounts (p. 8)

processed *(adjective)* prepared or changed by a series of steps (p. 10)

rain forest *(noun)* a tree-covered area that remains hot and wet throughout the year (p. 26)

reflex *(noun)* an automatic reaction that happens without your control (p. 18)

survive *(verb)* to continue to live or exist (p. 24)

theory *(noun)* an idea or a statement that explains how or why something happens (p. 22)

T. rex *(noun)* a large meat-eating dinosaur (p. 21)

triceratops *(noun)* a large plant-eating dinosaur with three horns (p. 21)

UFO *(noun)* an unidentified flying object (p. 30)

Index

25508

DATE DUE
